Don’t Be a Broke Adult

A money-savvy start for young people

By Edwin Palsma

First Printing, 2023

www.dontbeabrokeadult.com

Dedication

Writing a book is no small task. It involves hours of thinking, writing, rewriting, seeking feedback, revising again, designing, and much more. Going on the journey requires a very good reason because it's easy to never start, let alone finish.

For me, the motivation to begin and keep going came from my children, nephews, and nieces. I thought about what I could pass on to them that would genuinely make a difference and what insights could resonate and might guide them.

My expertise lies in a specific domain—money. While countless sources provide knowledge on budgeting, investing, saving, buying a house, and more, I felt there were two unexplored areas: M*indset* and E*motions*.

This book aims to guide you, Carson, Lexie, and Kaysha, on how to think about money and how to work with your emotions. Your chosen career, how much you earn or save, and where you end up; I have confidence that each of you will define your success uniquely. Within those choices, my ultimate goal is that you make smart decisions around money.

Table of Contents

Let's Begin...

First, let me tell you how to be a Broke Adult.

- Spend more than you earn!
- Try to keep up with your friends or your parents.
- Borrow money for fun things.
- Develop an addiction to drugs or alcohol.
- Be jealous.
- Be as inconsistent as possible.
- Blame everyone else (parents, society, government, friends, etc.) for all your problems.
- Don't waste time learning, don't read books, and don't listen to podcasts.
- Don't ask for help.
- Believe that you are smarter than everyone else.

Failing is easy...but success can also be easy. There is no trick, no magic, no 'one' answer, and no secret. If you are looking for a quick way to financial success, then this book won't be it because financial success takes time and patience (not fun, I know).

The way to be financially successful, other than blind luck, is to balance three things: M*indset*, E*motions,* and *Knowledge*.

<u>Knowledge</u> is learning how to budget, where to save, how to invest, how taxes work, and much more. There's a lot of books, articles, and podcasts where you can learn how money works. Many people think this is the only key to financial success but it's not.

Less commonly taught, and I'd argue more important, is learning to have the right Mindset and then learning how to interpret and regulate your Emotions.

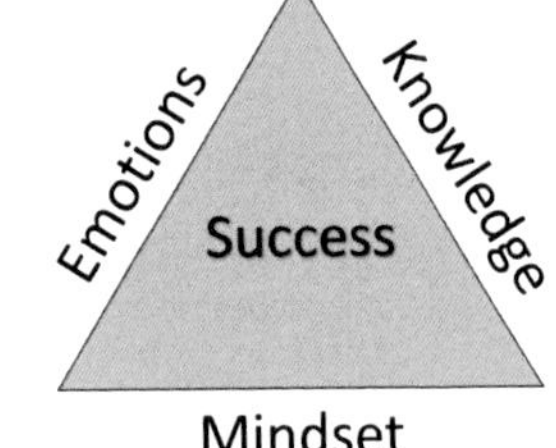

Mindset is having the right attitude, making good decisions, seeing your big picture, and understanding and making the right priorities for you.

Emotions is about recognizing why you feel as you do when topics of money comes up, embracing delayed gratification, curtailing jealousy, and fostering contentment.

Financial success takes time, it takes patience, and having the right perspective. Here's a short summary of the mindset and emotion points that I'll cover in the rest of the book.

- **Live Within Your Means**: Spend less than you earn.
- **Avoid Keeping Up with Others**: Don't try to keep up with friend's or family's spending habits.
- **Borrow Wisely**: Avoid borrowing money for non-essential, frivolous things.
- **Stay Clear of Addictions**: Developing an addiction to drugs or alcohol can severely hinder financial stability.
- **Cultivate Contentment**: Embrace contentment rather than jealousy.
- **Consistency is Key**: Strive for consistency in your habits.
- **Take Responsibility**: Avoid placing blame on external factors for your financial situation.
- **Invest in Knowledge**: Value learning, reading, and personal development.
- **Ask for Help**: Be open to seeking guidance when needed.
- **Stay Humble**: Acknowledge that you can always learn.

Quotes to Ponder

"It's so simple: you spend less than you earn. Invest shrewdly. Avoid toxic people and toxic activities. Try to keep learning all your life. And do a lot of deferred gratification. If you do all those things, you are almost certain to succeed. And if you don't, you'll need a lot of luck. And you don't want to need a lot of luck. You want to go into a game where you're very likely to win without having any unusual luck." – Charlie Munger, Warren Buffett's business partner

Mindset

Achieving Financial Success: A Roadmap

While brilliance and luck can play a role, most financially successful individuals get there through hard work and consistent, wise decisions. If you're reading this, you likely have an interest in financial matters and the determination to succeed. Let's start with some philosophical perspectives to set the right Mindset.

- **Money is Behavior-Driven**: Money isn't just about numbers; it's about your behaviors, decisions, and the mistakes you avoid.
- **Make a Positive Contribution**: Our society thrives when individuals contribute positively. Find a way to make a meaningful impact in your chosen field. Be useful.
- **Understand our Economic System**: In Canada, you're rewarded for your contributions. As you acquire skills and take on more valuable roles, your financial situation will improve from surviving to thriving.
- **Embrace Financial Planning**: The future is uncertain, so it's essential to save and invest. Savings provide financial security and flexibility for various life situations.
- **Focus on What You Can Control**: You can control your attitude, work ethic, spending habits, who you associate with, and willingness to learn. You can care about broader issues like taxes and politics but concentrate your energy on what you can directly influence for more significant results.

My belief is that there are two fundamental keys to the right mindset in achieving success in life and personal finances. The first is genuine self-awareness. Not who we wish or think we are, but a candid, precise, and honest understanding of our true selves. Financially, this is having a comprehensive grasp of what you own, the extent of your debts, the motivations driving your purchasing decisions, your financial fears, your aspirations, and the extent to which you're willing to make sacrifices.

The second key to success hinges on recognizing and embracing your agency, which is your capacity to make decisions. You are not solely at the mercy of external circumstances. While you cannot alter your past, you do possess the power to shape your future. You can make choices that either propel you towards a more favorable position or set you back. You have a degree of control, and hold the reins in determining how you'll exercise that control.

With all these philosophies in mind, let's dive into practical strategies for achieving the right mindset.

Quotes to Ponder

"Rich people have big libraries and small TVs. Poor people have big TVs and small libraries." – Zig Ziglar, motivational speaker

"Early to bed and early to rise, makes a man healthy, wealthy and wise." – Benjamin Franklin, American philosopher, inventor and Founding Father

"Doing well with money isn't necessarily about what you know. It's about how you behave. And behaviour is really hard to teach, even to really smart people." – Morgan Housel, author of The Psychology of Money

Decisions and Luck

One bright day in late autumn, a family of ants was bustling about in the warm sunshine, drying the grain they'd stored up over the summer. A starving grasshopper, a violin under his arm, came up and humbly begged for a bite to eat.

"What!" cried the ants in surprise, "Haven't you stored anything away for the winter? What in the world were you doing this summer?"

"I didn't have time to store food," whined the grasshopper; "I was so busy making music and playing with my friends that before I knew it, the summer was gone."

The ants shrugged their shoulders in disgust.

"Making music? Playing with your friends?" they cried. "Very well; here's one meal for tonight but be off with you." And they turned their backs on the grasshopper and went on with their work. "There's a time for work and a time for play."

In my role as a financial advisor, I've had the privilege of assisting and meeting thousands of individuals. One striking observation is that while some of the financially successful have had fortunate breaks, the majority have diligently worked to accumulate their wealth. Like in the fable above, the decisions you make will have consequences. Every ordinary moment of your life is an opportunity to make the future easier or harder.

The Formula:

Decisions + Luck = Your Financial Outcomes

The most significant decision you'll make is how you choose to spend or save your money. No one will force you to buy a specific car, pursue a university degree, or take annual Hawaiian vacations. The power of choice lies firmly in your hands, and it significantly influences your financial journey.

Next, consider how you allocate your time. Balance is key; you can't work all the time, nor can you completely abstain from it. Striking the right mix between work (including studying, learning, and earning) and leisure (relaxation, enjoying life, and spending) significantly shapes your financial outcomes.

Certain decisions expand your future possibilities. Graduating from high school and pursuing higher education, maintaining a healthy savings account, and acquiring new skills open doors to diverse opportunities. Conversely, certain decisions can constrain your future, such as reckless driving or accumulating debt through extravagant spending.

To enhance your odds of financial success, channel your time and energy into the right pursuits. Be proactive and deliberate in the aspects of life that you can control. Don’t spend energy on worrying or trying to alter circumstances beyond your control.

The Goal: Financial Maturity

It's common for young individuals to prioritize short-term considerations. However, true financial success demands long-term thinking and delayed gratification.

Here's a straightforward framework to guide your daily decisions:

- **Live Within Your Means**: Spend only what you have.
- **Dedicate Yourself to Excellence**: Work diligently, whether it's in school or your profession.
- **Seek Opportunities for Progress**: Continuously look for avenues to advance, be it by securing a better job, acquiring additional knowledge through courses, or nurturing relationships with successful individuals.
- **Cultivate a Savings Habit**: Commit to saving a portion of your income every year.
- **Get Wise Counsel**: Seek advice from knowledgeable individuals.

By adhering to these principles, you'll not only make sound decisions but also chart a course toward financial well-being.

Quotes to Ponder

"A lot of success in life happens by avoiding making the big mistakes." – Author Unknown

"Instead of focusing on how to get rich, focus on not ending up poor and you will have more success in life." – Charlie Munger, wealthy investor and Warren Buffett's business partner

Gain a Larger Perspective

In ancient times, a wise man presented a unique challenge to six blind individuals. He asked them to encircle a massive beast and describe it in detail. Each blind person approached the task differently. The first one, grasping the trunk, confidently proclaimed it was a great snake. The second, hugging a leg, likened it to a sturdy tree. The third, holding the tail, exclaimed it was a rope. The fourth, touching an ear, compared it to a grand fan. The fifth, feeling a tusk, believed it was a large spear. Lastly, the sixth blind person, examining the massive side of the creature, was convinced it was a solid wall. An intense argument ensued. The wise man intervened, explaining that while each person's perspective was valid within their assigned area, none had the overall perspective needed to accurately describe the elephant in its entirety.

Now, let's dig into something philosophical once more.

One of the most significant financial mistakes I observe is making "today" choices when you should be making "tomorrow" choices.

Obvious Tomorrow Choices

- How much should I save from my paycheck?
- Should I pursue higher education, and if so, which institution?
- Should I commit to marriage or remain single?

Today Choices that are actually Tomorrow Choices (Hint: This Is Crucial)

- Should I opt for a salad or indulge in French Fries today?
- Should I hit the gym or spend the evening watching TV?
- Should I put in some overtime at work?
- Should I discuss a potential raise with my boss?

The first category of questions can usually be resolved by weighing the pros and cons to arrive at the right answer, or at least a good one.

However, the last category is deceptive. We may believe we are making a minor 'today' decision, but these accumulated 'today' choices ultimately shape our 'tomorrow' outcomes. Exercising today won't make you instantly fit and healthy, but consistently exercising (or not) will significantly impact your future well-being.

It's one of the hardest things to do...make a decision or take an action today where the benefits aren't seen for weeks, or even years. The most successful people I know are amazing at this one skill.

In essence, much like the fable mentioned earlier, thinking that you are only making a 'today' choice (akin to seeing the elephant as merely a wall when it's much more) might, in fact, be a 'tomorrow' choice. It's crucial to take a step back or seek advice from others to gain a broader perspective.

Quotes to Ponder

"Nothing is more difficult, and therefore more precious, than to be able to decide." – Napoleon Bonaparte

"Decision making is easy when your values are clear." – Roy Disney

"Life is about choices. Some we regret, some we're proud of. Some will haunt us forever. The message: we are what we chose to be." – Graham Brown, American fiction author

"The quality of your life is built on the quality of your decisions." – Wesam Fawzi, business and life coach

Achieve Balance

Once upon a time, a squirrel served a lion — the details of this service are lost to history, but one thing was certain: the squirrel had earned the favor of the lion, no small accomplishment. In return for his service, the lion promised the squirrel a wagonload of nuts upon the completion of his duties.

Promises were made, but time continued to pass swiftly. The squirrel often grappled with hunger while maintaining a cheerful facade in the presence of his master, tears often welling up in his eyes. When he glanced around the forest, he would occasionally spot his squirrel friends high up in the trees. The squirrel could only watch, for he was perpetually toiling for the lion.

Finally, the squirrel grew old and became a burden to the lion. It was time for his retirement, and true to his word, the lion granted him the promised wagonload of nuts — splendid nuts, like none ever seen before. Unfortunately, the squirrel had lost all his teeth long ago.

The tale of the squirrel serves as a lesson in balance. The squirrel was so focused on the distant future that he missed the joys of the present. For us, achieving balance means balancing our commitments to family, health, sleep, spirituality, recreation, work, and finances. But how do we strike that balance?

Brian Dyson, the former president and CEO of Coca-Cola, once said: "*Imagine life as a game in which you are juggling five balls in the air. They are called – Work, Family, Health, Friends, and Spirit.*

You will soon understand that Work is a rubber ball. If you drop it, it will bounce back. But the other four Balls – Family, Health, Friends, and Spirit – are made of glass. If you drop one of these, they will be irrevocably scuffed, marked, nicked, damaged, or even shattered. They will never be the same."

Balancing life doesn't mean you should never focus. Sometimes we must seize opportunities and concentrate on one aspect of our lives. But, like the squirrel, we may become so engrossed in work that we lose sight of the rest, or we might focus solely on having fun and forget to prepare for the future, like the grasshopper in an earlier chapter.

A balanced life involves enjoying the present and preparing for the future. Some possessions and experiences are worth having because they enhance our enjoyment of life, such as baseball gloves, sewing machines, Pokémon cards, earrings, and experiences like sharing a coffee with a friend, traveling to Europe, or skiing. Enjoying life is essential; otherwise, what's the point?

However, it's also crucial to plan and prepare for the future. Some of the things you buy can be considered investments that grow or enable you to earn more money in the future. These might include a house, investments in businesses, or books that expand your knowledge. Even your sewing machine can become a good investment if it generates income for you.

Similarly, some experiences serve as investments, like attending post-secondary school to earn a degree or certificate, traveling to broaden your perspective, or attending a seminar to acquire new skills.

If you spend all your money on non-investment items, your future self may wish you had been more forward-thinking. Conversely, if you focus solely on investments, you may become wealthy but potentially lead a joyless life. The key is balance — don't lean too heavily in one direction or the other.

Quotes to Ponder

"Life is like riding a bicycle. To keep your balance, you must keep moving." – Albert Einstein

"There is no such thing as work-life balance. There are work-life choices, and you make them, and they have consequences." – Jack Welch, former CEO of General Electric

"There is no decision that we can make that doesn't come with some sort of balance or sacrifice." – Simon Sinek, motivational speaker

90,000 Hours

In ancient times, the great Library of Alexandria burned, and it's said that only one book survived. This book wasn't particularly valuable, so a man who could read a little bought it for a few pennies. Inside, he discovered a tiny note containing the secret of the 'Touchstone.'

The Touchstone was a small pebble that could turn any common metal into pure gold. The note explained that the real Touchstone was among thousands of other pebbles on the shore, all looking exactly the same. The difference was that the real one would feel warm, while ordinary pebbles were cold. The man decided to find the Touchstone.

He sold his belongings, bought supplies, camped on the seashore, and began testing pebbles. Days turned into weeks, and weeks into months. He formed a habit of throwing pebbles into the sea, discarding them if they were cold. One day, he picked up a warm pebble, but out of habit, he still threw it away.

For some of us, work can feel like mindless repetition, like throwing pebbles into the sea. However, it's crucial to maintain the right perspective to seize opportunities.

The average person works around 90,000 hours in their lifetime, from the age of 20 to 65. Making $20 per hour, you'll earn $1,800,000 over your life. Therefore, you have that amount of money to spend and save throughout your life.

One way to ease the pressure of making money is to spend less. You can also work more hours, take on overtime, or get a second job to increase your income. Another approach is to work longer into your 70s or 80s, spreading your working hours over a longer period of time.

You can also aim to make more money per hour. Earning $40 an hour, you'd only need to work 45,000 hours to reach the same financial goal if you keep your spending in check.

In essence, you have a limited number of hours and a finite earning potential. If you make more money per hour or work extra hours, you will get closer to your financial objectives.

Rule one is to avoid overspending, as discussed earlier. Rule two is to find ways to increase your income, allowing you to have more to spend or retire earlier.

So when you think about working part-time during high school, summers, or university, remember that every hour worked brings you closer to those 90,000 hours.

Extra Credit:

If you can find a job where you're paid for your output or creativity, rather than by the hour, you'll gain flexibility and potentially earn more. Jobs that pay by output include graphic design, consulting, writing, and owning a business. While you'll still need to work hard, there's potential for more flexibility, which for some means a more enjoyable life.

Quotes to Ponder

"Failure is not the opposite of success: it's part of success." – Arianna Huffington, businesswoman

"Quality means doing it right when no one is looking." – Henry Ford, businessman

"The difference between ordinary and extraordinary is that little extra." – Jimmy Johnson, football player

"Every accomplishment starts with the decision to try." – John F Kennedy, US President

"Be humble. Be hungry. And always be the hardest worker in the room." – Dwayne "The Rock" Johnson, entertainer

"Work hard and be kind and amazing things will happen." – Conan O'Brien, comedian

"Opportunity is missed by most people because it is dressed in overalls and looks like work." – Thomas Edison, Inventor

Maximize your Earning Potential

The Mice once had a meeting to devise a plan to free themselves from their adversary, the Cat. They sought a way to know when she was approaching, allowing them time to escape. Living in constant fear of her claws, they scarcely dared venture out of their dens, whether by day or night.

Numerous plans were discussed, but none seemed good enough. Finally, a very young Mouse stood up and proposed a seemingly simple yet potentially successful plan.

"All we need to do is hang a bell around the Cat's neck. When we hear the bell ringing, we will instantly know that our enemy is approaching."

The Mice were taken aback, realizing they had not thought of such a plan before. However, amidst their celebration of this newfound strategy, an elderly Mouse rose and posed a crucial question:

"I must say that the young Mouse's plan is quite ingenious. But let me ask this: Who will bell the Cat?"

This story serves as a reminder that while good ideas and dreams are inspiring, execution is the key to turning dreams into reality. Simply desiring wealth is not enough; you must take action.

In essence, there are only two ways to make money; through labour (you working) or from capital (owning investments that make money). Hoping to inherit or win the lottery is not a reliable source of income.

Labour entails having a job and receiving payment for your efforts. It requires you to provide value and be of service to someone else in exchange for compensation. Work can be physical, such as landscaping or waiting tables, or intellectual, like writing or managing people.

One piece of advice is to perform the work of the job you want, not the job you currently hold. This extra effort won't guarantee an immediate raise, but it shows your worth to your employer, positioning you as a strong candidate for future opportunities.

The second way to make money, and ultimately become wealthy, is by owning income-generating investments. This allows your investments to work for you, creating passive income. Starting with labor, you can use your earnings to acquire assets that generate income over time.

Income-generating assets can be rental properties, farms that produce crops, or profitable businesses. While some assets provide immediate income, others may appreciate in value over time, leading to potential profits when sold.

In the beginning, focus on acquiring assets that generate income. Once you accumulate enough of these assets, the income they generate can fund your desired lifestyle.

Quotes to Ponder

"Making money is easy. It is. The difficult thing in life is in keeping it." – John McAfee, computer programmer and businessman

"Too many people spend money they haven't earned, to buy things they don't want, to impress people they don't like." – Will Rogers, Actor

Emotions

Get to Know Future You

> *Once upon a time, a farmer discovered an extraordinary egg in his goose's nest. This egg shone with a brilliant, golden hue and felt as heavy as lead. Initially, the farmer suspected a trick, but he took the egg home and soon realized it was pure gold. Each morning, the goose laid another golden egg, and the farmer grew wealthy by selling them. Over time, his wealth fueled his greed, and he hatched a plan to get all the gold at once. He killed the goose, only to find nothing inside.*

The root of most financial mistakes is letting your emotions make your financial decisions. We all have emotions and we come by them honestly. Everything our parents have ever said, the financial conditions we experienced when we were young, and our genetics all play a role in the emotions we experience when it comes to money. Does money make you anxious, inspired, greedy, frustrated, angry, motivated, etc.?

Learning to recognize our emotions and where they come from is the first step to not letting emotions drive your financial ship. You can't ignore them but you can make decisions that will help you succeed in spite of them.

The most common emotion that causes financial mistakes is impatience. It's focusing on desires and acquiring material possessions when you don't have the money. Just like the farmer who owned the Golden Goose and wasn't satisfied with what he had, we often jeopardize our financial future (our ability to earn income and save) by burdening it with debt. Patience is a virtue, and it can yield significant rewards.

Money typically comes from two sources: earning it (through a job or investments) or borrowing from your future self.

You will eventually pay for everything. The question is whether you want to pay for it now (as Today You) or later (as Future You). When you make a purchase with money you don't currently have (by using a credit card or borrowing from your parents), it's Future You who will foot the bill.

Now, imagine asking Future You, "Do you want to pay for this item right now and postpone other financial goals?" Would 30-year-old you want to be paying off the Europe trip that 20-year-old you took? Would 35-year-old you still want to be tackling the student loan for a university degree? Would 45-year-old you want to have a mortgage payment for the house you bought earlier?

Financial maturity is the ability to make good financial decisions over time. Maturity involves recognizing that each choice carries a compounding effect; buying something today means less money for something else tomorrow. You can't have it all.

As I often tell my kids, I have the ability to buy almost anything I desire (within reason, of course—I'm not a billionaire). I can buy nearly any new car or go on any global vacation. However, I can't buy everything I want. There's always a limit and so I have to prioritize some things over others.

Likely, you also have limited resources, so you can't afford everything. Every purchase means having less money to spend on something else. Thus, it's essential to carefully consider your spending choices and whether they outweigh future needs.

Quotes to Ponder

"Spending is quick. Earning is slow." – Russian Proverb

"Spending money to show people how much you have is the fastest way to have less money." – Morgan Housel, author of The Psychology of Money

"Be happy when you work, thankful when you earn, cautious when you spend, shrewd when you save, and charitable when you give." – Matshona Dhliwayo, Canadian author of The Little Book of Inspiration

Why Saving Matters

One summer, Johnny had a chance to earn some extra money by picking blackberries and selling them to his neighbor, who ran a local bakery and used them for pies. On a particular evening, he stumbled upon a hidden bush behind a ditch and managed to fill two 5-gallon pails in just 30 minutes.

"Tonight, I'm going to treat myself to Menchies Ice Cream, a Mars bar, and buy some new hockey cards," he whispered to himself, the anticipation making his mouth water.

Lost in his daydream, Johnny tripped over a branch on the path and fell into the ditch, spilling all the blackberries into the mud. He sat there, disheartened, as his dreams of treats washed away.

Just because you dream of something you want (like Johnny) doesn't mean you have it. And that's why you need to save.

First, let me re-introduce you to an important concept: 'Future You.'

Future You is still you, just older – perhaps 10 years or even 40 years older. What do you think Future You might say when looking back at Today You? Probably things like "eat well," "take care of your body," and "make good financial decisions." One of those financial decisions will likely be that you should have saved more.

There are six important thing you'll need to save up for:

- **Unexpected Emergencies**: Costs like braces, extended periods of unemployment after losing a job or sustaining an injury, new tires for your car, or replacing your house's furnace.
- **A Car**: If you lack access to public transit, a car becomes essential for getting to work.
- **Education**: While not everyone needs post-secondary education, you might decide to upgrade your skills or pursue a university education later on. Without savings, this could lead to student loans and future financial burdens.
- **A Home**: Even if homeownership isn't your goal, saving for a down payment is still wise. It offers financial security, allowing you to buy property in a more affordable area or potentially invest in real estate for the future.
- **Retirement**: Although some may find careers they love and never want to retire, most people will want to slow down or fully retire at some point. Saving 10% of your income each month from a young age can pave the way for a comfortable retirement.
- **Legacy**: If you have children or want to leave a financial legacy for a charity or family, setting money aside is essential. Achieving this goal takes time and careful planning with the assistance of a lawyer or financial advisor to maximize your intended gifts.

All six savings goals involve setting aside money for the future, and the best way to save is to work hard and spend wisely.

Quotes to Ponder

"Monthly income of $2,000 with monthly expenses of $1,500 - result Happiness. Monthly income $2,000 with monthly expenses of $2,500 - result Misery." – credit to Charles Dickens.

Four Emotional Roadblocks

Once upon a time, a little hungry mouse discovered its way into a basket filled with tempting corn. It had to squeeze itself through a narrow opening between the strips of the basket. Despite the challenge, the mouse was determined to reach the corn. When it finally succeeded, it indulged itself to the point of bursting. In fact, it became about three times as wide around its middle as when it first entered!

Eventually, the mouse felt satiated and attempted to exit. However, it could only manage to get its head out. It sat there, groaning and moaning from both the discomfort inside and its eagerness to escape the basket. At that moment, a weasel passed by and quickly grasped the situation.

"My friend," the weasel said, "I understand what you've been up to. You've been overindulging, and this is the consequence. You'll have to remain there until you shrink back to the size you were when you entered!"

Much like the mouse, if we allow our decisions to be solely driven by emotions, we may find ourselves trapped in undesirable situations. To achieve financial success, it's crucial to be aware of four common emotional biases or reactions.

Certainty Bias: People generally prefer certainty over uncertainty. The discomfort of not knowing can be unsettling. From a financial perspective, wealth tends to grow more rapidly when invested in growing businesses rather than just placing it in a GIC (Guaranteed Investment Certificate). However, because the future of a business is uncertain, many shy away from such investments in favor of lower but more certain returns in the short run.

Availability Heuristic: Our minds tend to focus on recent or dramatic events. For example, most people fear sharks more than mosquitoes, even though mosquitoes cause significantly more fatalities. Media outlets often emphasize dramatic news, promoting doom and gloom, which can lead investors to make poor decisions. History shows that patient, long-term thinking usually yields better results.

Loss Aversion: This bias is that losing a dollar has a more emotional impact than gaining that same dollar. People tend to gravitate towards surefire investments like bank accounts and GICs because they are perceived as safe, even though they may lose value due to inflation. As a young investor with time on your side, achieving better returns can significantly accelerate the growth of your wealth.

Overconfidence Bias: This bias involves overestimating one's abilities. It can manifest as being overconfident in your job performance or overly certain about an investment's outcome, either positively or negatively. Managing money isn't an exact science, and many factors are random or lucky. Recognizing this bias is crucial to avoiding costly mistakes.

Over the past 40 years, numerous studies have shown that investors in the stock market often buy and sell at the wrong times due to emotional influences. When things seem bad, they sell their investments instead of buying at low prices. Or when things are good, they pay too much for the investments they buy.

Even experienced investors deal with these biases, but they are better at recognizing and mitigating them.

One easy rule of thumb. Save like a pessimist and invest like an optimist.

Quotes to Ponder

"It is an acknowledged fact that we perceive errors in the work of others more readily than in our own." – Leonardo da Vinci

"If there's something you really want to believe, that's what you should question the most." – Penn Jillette from Penn and Teller

"To invest successfully over a lifetime does not require a stratospheric IQ or unusual business insights. What's needed is a sound intellectual framework for making decisions and the ability to keep emotions from corroding that framework." – Warren Buffett

Be Thankful, Generous, and Humble

A slave named Androcles once escaped from his master and fled to the forest. As he was wandering about he came upon a Lion lying on the ground, moaning and groaning. At first he turned to flee, but finding that the Lion did not pursue him, he turned back and went up to him. As he came near, the Lion put out his paw, which was swollen and bleeding. Androcles found that a huge thorn had gotten into it and was causing all the pain.

He pulled out the thorn and bound up the paw of the Lion, who was soon able to rise and lick the hand of Androcles like a dog. Then the Lion took Androcles to his cave, and every day he brought him meat to eat. But shortly afterwards, both Androcles and the Lion were captured, and the slave was sentenced to be fed to the Lion after the latter had been kept without food for several days.

The Emperor and his Court came to see the spectacle, and Androcles was led out into the middle of the arena. Soon the Lion was let loose from his den and rushed bounding and roaring towards his victim. But as soon as he came near to Androcles he recognized his friend, and fawned upon him, licking Androcles's hands like a friendly dog.

The Emperor, surprised at this, summoned Androcles, who told him the whole story, whereupon the slave was pardoned and freed, and the Lion let loose to his native forest.

There are three more important things that make a difference but not in how much money you'll make. Instead, they will shape the kind of person you'll be.

First, you're super lucky! You can read, someone got you this book, and you live in one of the most peaceful times in history. Plus, you have lots of choices ahead. Things might be tough, but the world is full of opportunities for those who set their mind to pursuing them. So, be thankful, not entitled or a victim.

Second, because you'll have it better than some others, be generous. Sharing and helping others keeps you thinking about the big world, not just your own success. Whether you believe in karma or not, people who share are often more successful. It's because generous people usually see the world as full of opportunity. They also attract like minded people in their life, thereby feeding off of each other.

Lastly, be humble. We're all successful because of the people around us—parents, teachers, friends, bosses, and more. None of us does it alone. We're all part of a team, and it's easier to succeed when we work together.

Quotes to Ponder

"Some people are always grumbling because roses have thorns; I am thankful that thorns have roses." – Alphonse Karr, French author

Knowledge

Taxes - How They Work

One day, a farmer's son was grumbling about the never-ending task of cleaning the barn. "Every day, it's the same routine – shovel, haul, dump. Shovel, haul, dump. Why do I have to deal with all this manure!" he exclaimed.

Overhearing his son's complaints, the father explained, "Well, son, we make our living by raising cows and selling their milk. It's how we provide for our home, cars, and food. But, as you know, life isn't all sunshine and roses. Cleaning up the manure is just one of the responsibilities that comes with running a farm."

Much like the farmer's son, we'd love to earn money without the work. It would be ideal if someone else could handle the manure while we reap all the rewards from selling the milk.

However, that's not how life works. When you earn money, taxes are your contribution to the greater good, funding essential services like schools, hospitals, and infrastructure.

Don't stress too much about the taxes you pay. You'll never end up paying more in taxes than you earn. Every time you earn a dollar (every single time), you'll always keep a significant portion of it. This is something many people misunderstand. They might hesitate to work harder for fear of higher taxes. But think of taxes as a necessary by-product of making money, much like the manure on a farm.

In Canada, there are two main types of taxes:

- **Consumption Taxes**: These are the taxes you pay when you make purchases (e.g., PST, GST, property taxes, liquor taxes). If you want to pay less in consumption taxes, simply buy fewer things.
- **Income Tax**: This is the larger portion of your tax bill and is often misunderstood. First, income taxes are based on the calendar year, with all your income from various sources added together for your total yearly income. Also, income taxes are progressive, meaning the more you earn, the higher the tax rate, but only on that higher income.

Many Canadians think that if you go into a higher tax bracket, you pay more taxes on all your income, which isn't true. An example explains it best.

In Canada, if you earn $12,000 or less in a year, you won't owe any income taxes. If you make $20,000 a year, you still don't pay taxes on the first $12,000, but only on the $8,000 you earn above that; on that $8,000 you will pay 20% in taxes, totaling $1,600.

If you go on to make $60,000 a year, you will still pay zero taxes on the first $12,000 and 20% on the income from $12,000 to $50,000. And then you will pay 30% on the income over $50,000 (on the $10,000). This progressive tax rate continues as you earn more, with higher percentages applied to higher income levels.

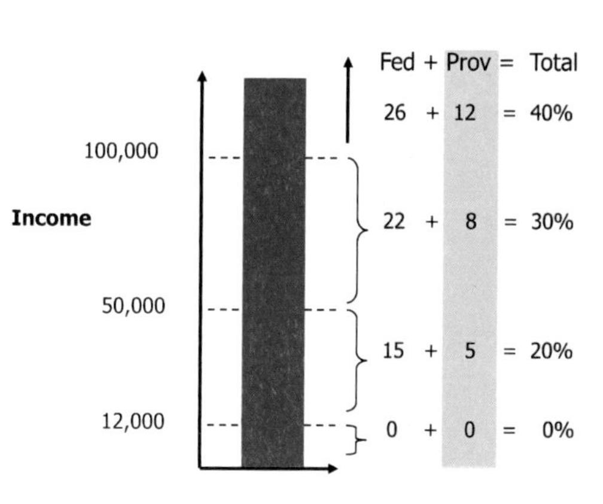

Paying a substantial amount in taxes is a positive indicator of financial success. So, my hope for you is that you pay a lot of taxes each year!

My best advice to you is to prioritize making money overpaying less taxes. When your income exceeds $50,000 a year, consider consulting an accountant or financial advisor to explore strategies for minimizing taxes. Until then, it's not a concern worth losing sleep over.

Quotes to Ponder

"Don't worry about being famous or making money; the most important thing is being the best you can be. You have to become a master of your craft, and everything else will work out." – Anastasia Soare, wealthy entrepreneur

Inflation: The Silent Erosion

Once in a distant land, there was a diligent farmer preparing for a journey to the town to sell his assortment of goods. His trusty camel was loaded with milk, eggs, and meat, all neatly secured. As he stood there, admiring his packed camel, a thought crossed his mind. Straw, being exceedingly light, could surely find a place atop the camel's burden. With this notion, he carefully placed a few bales of straw on the camel's back. Regrettably, the straw, though light in isolation, proved too much for the camel, leading to a catastrophic fall and the infamous saying, 'the straw that broke the camel's back.'

Inflation, in many ways, resembles that seemingly lightweight straw. It is the gradual increase in the cost of goods and services over time. These incremental changes often go unnoticed in the short term, much like the weight of each additional straw on the camel's back. However, when viewed through the lens of an extended period, the cumulative impact becomes strikingly evident, akin to the farmer's overloaded camel.

Consider the cost of gasoline as an example. On a month-to-month basis, the price hikes may not appear significant, but over the course of three decades, the aggregated rise is substantial:

Year	Cost of Gas in Vancouver
1990	$0.40
2000	$0.70
2010	$1.20
2020	$1.70

This trend extends to other facets of life, including the escalating costs of homes, food, and various essentials. While certain items, like TVs, computers, entertainment, etc., experience price decreases due to technological advancements, others continue to increase in cost.

To combat the relentless impact of inflation, it is important that your savings grow over time. Consider this scenario: if you diligently save $10,000 at the age of 20 but opt to stow it away in your bedroom, by the time you reach 60, its purchasing power would have significantly diminished. That same $10,000 would only be capable of buying a quarter of what it once could. To keep its value, that $10,000 would need to grow to at least $40,000.

This underscores the critical importance of mastering the art of investing your money well. To outpace inflation, one must invest in assets that grow at a rate higher than the pace of inflation itself. In doing so, you shield your financial future from the relentless encroachment of rising costs, ensuring your long-term prosperity.

Quotes to Ponder

"Inflation makes the wealthiest people richer and the regular people poorer." – James Cook, English philosopher

Types of Savings Accounts: Where to Safeguard your Money

Once upon a time, a young girl was entrusted with the daily task of collecting eggs from their family's chickens. Her parents had a simple rule: Collect only twelve eggs at a time and transport them out of the barn before returning for another dozen.

One fateful day, in a bit of haste, she decided to carry four egg cartons at once. As she carefully made her way out of the chicken coop, her dog suddenly attempted to enter the coop! Startled, the door swung sharply open , knocking her arm, and she dropped all the cartons, resulting in cracked eggs.

Much like our young egg collector, you need a safe place to put your saved money. As a young individual, you probably started with a piggy bank and eventually opened a bank account. But what comes next?

First and foremost, give each dollar a designated purpose. Some will be for spending, while others will be reserved for long-term goals, such as a new car or retirement. As in the story above, putting all your eggs in one basket is not a recipe for success. Different types of accounts serve distinct purposes, so you will eventually need several of them.

To simplify, there are five primary categories where you can park your money. Banks may use different names for them, or you might have multiple accounts serving similar functions. However, in Canada, they generally fall into these five categories:

- **Chequing Account**: This account is for regular inflow and outflow of money. Your paychecks get deposited here, and you use it for spending, whether through your debit card, online payments, or cheques. Maintaining at least $1,000 in this account at all times is advisable to avoid fees. However, it won't earn you much, if any income.
- **Savings Account**: When you start accumulating more than $1,000, the bank will encourage you to consider a savings account. Here, you'll earn a modest amount of interest, usually in the 1-3% range, depending on the economic cycle. This is where you save money for moderately larger expenses, such as your first car, unexpected car repairs, university costs, a wedding dress, a vacation, etc. Note that you'll pay minimal taxes on the interest earned in this account.
- **Tax-Free Savings Account (TFSA)**: Once you have funds in your savings account that you intend to keep for more than six months, consider transferring them to a Tax-Free Savings Account. While your parents might use this account for retirement savings, it's also a great place for young individuals to save for significant purchases like cars and homes. Earnings in a TFSA are tax-free.
- **Registered Retirement Savings Plan (RRSP)**: This is where you save for retirement, possibly many years in the future. Consider contributing to an RRSP if your annual income exceeds $50,000. If you earn less, a TFSA might be a more suitable option.
- **First Home Savings Account (FHSA)**: In Canada, this account allows you to save for your first home. You can contribute $8,000 per year for five years. You won't pay taxes on contributions or withdrawals from this account.

Deciding where to save, how to transfer money between accounts, and when to make these transfers can be an ongoing process. Seek guidance from someone knowledgeable about finances, such as a parent, aunt or uncle, friend's parents, or a financial advisor, to help you navigate these decisions. Initially, it might seem daunting, but with practice, it becomes second nature. Remember, it's always better to seek help and ask questions than to make costly mistakes.

Quotes to Ponder

"Don't be afraid to ask questions. Don't be afraid to ask for help when you need it. I do that every day. Asking for help isn't a sign of weakness, it's a sign of strength. It shows you have the courage to admit when you don't know something, and to learn something new." – Barack Obama

Money Making Money

> *Once upon a time, a Crow, half-dead with thirst, stumbled upon a Pitcher that had once held water. Unfortunately, only a small amount of water remained at the bottom, and the Crow couldn't reach it with its beak. It tried and tried but eventually had to give up in despair. Then, an idea struck the Crow. It began dropping pebbles into the Pitcher, one by one, until the water level rose enough for the Crow to quench its thirst and save its life.*

Getting money to grow is not instantaneous. It's a gradual process, much like the Crow putting stones in the Pitcher. Little by little, you make progress.

Money grows because other people want to use it and will pay you for the privilege of using your money.

Here are two examples.

If I had $100, I could buy boxes of gum from Costco and then sell the individual packages. Let's assume I can sell the individual packages for twice as much as I paid for them when I bought them in bulk...then I would have a profit of $100 at the end of the day. But if I don't have the $100 to start, I could borrow the money from you and we would share some of the $100 profit (because you put in the money and I put in the work of buying and then selling the gum).

You have to decide how much risk you want to take. If you are worried that I won't be able to sell the gum, then maybe you ask for just an interest payment back. You will give me the $100 but at the end of the day, you want to get $105 dollars back. Then, if I'm unsuccessful and don't sell all the gum, you will still have made $5. I take on the risk and you get certainty. Maybe you are not even sure I'll make my money back so you ask to hold onto my bike as collateral...so if I don't even make the $100 back, you can sell my bike and get your money back.

If you think I will be successful, then you can agree to share in the profits instead. At the end of the day, you get your money back and we share the profits 50/50 but with no guarantees that you will make money.

In the first case, you are loaning me money and because you want less uncertainty, you accept a lower rate of return.

In the second case, you are taking on some ownership of our little business and will have uncertainty on how much money we make, but you will potentially make more money.

And this is how money grows...you loan money to someone (friend, bank, business) and they pay you a fixed amount of money back. Or you partner with someone and share in the profits depending how the business does.

In the real world, loaning money is like investing in a GIC, term deposit, or high interest savings account (loans to a bank) or a bond (loan to a business). You are getting more certainty in the returns, but you will get lower returns over time.

Being a business owner will give you more uncertainty, but a higher return on your money if the business is successful.

In the real world, there are millions of businesses out there that need money. They need money to buy inventory to sell (like the gum in our example), to rent out a building (to build things, have a restaurant, or sell knick knacks), or to pay employees (to build things, come up with new inventions, etc.).

You can also invest in a building to rent out to others to live in or to run their businesses out of them.

At the end of the day, where you decide to invest your money will have an impact on how much money you will make. If you find good businesses that are profitable over time (and time is key), then that's the best place to invest. You can start your own business, join with friends, or invest in businesses that have already been created.

When investing in other businesses, the stock market is where you can find thousands of companies that are already established. By becoming a part owner of one, you'll share in their profits. Companies like Amazon, Google, Royal Bank, and Canadian Tire have consistently grown and enriched many investors. Nevertheless, there have been failures like Enron, Nortel, Pets.com, and Kodak. The challenge is to pick winners rather than losers. Over time, the overall stock market has consistently shown growth. While there are periods of volatility over days, months, and even years, history has demonstrated that staying invested for at least five years and selecting profitable businesses (or seeking expert guidance) can lead to strong returns.

When starting on this journey, ask for help! There's bound to be people in your life who have gone down this path before and would love to help you out.

Quotes to Ponder

"I've never met a rich pessimist." – Ned Goodman, Canadian investor and founder of Dynamic Funds.

"Failure is not to be feared. It is from failure that most growth comes." – Dee Hock, founder of VISA.

The Power of Compounding: Unleashing the Eighth Wonder of the World

Imagine a scenario posed by a professor at UBC: "Would you prefer I give you $33,000 every day for 31 days, or would you rather start with a single penny today, doubling it each day for 31 days? You'll have two pennies on day 2, four pennies on day 3, and so forth. Which option would you choose?"

Compounding, often dubbed the "eighth wonder of the world," can best be understood through an example. Let's say you have an investment that grows at a steady 10% annually. If you began with $100, it would grow to $110 after one year. So, how long would it take for your initial $100 to transform into $200?

At first glance, the simple math suggests 10 years – you'd earn $10 each year. However, in the second year, something magical happens. You earn $10.10. Why? You're not just earning interest on your original $100; you're also earning on the $10 earned in the first year, including an extra dime. This compounding effect accelerates the growth of your wealth. At a 10% annual return, your money would actually double in just 7.2 years!

To make this process more accessible, there's a handy math trick known as "The Rule of 72." Divide your rate of return into 72, and you'll discover how long it takes for your money to double. In this case, 10% into 72 reveals that it takes 7.2 years.

Why is this concept vital? Because it illustrates how savings can grow faster than you might anticipate due to compounding.

Consider a practical example: An 18-year-old decides to save $2,000 a year but only saves for 10 years. They decide to invest in the stock market and end up earning an average of 7% a year. They will have saved $20,000 but by the time they reach 65, the money has grown to $360,000 because of compounding.

Now, their twin sibling decides to wait and starts saving $2,000 a year at age 27, instead of age 18, but then saves continuously until age 65 (38 years). Who wins? Assuming the same 7% rate of return, they both end up with around $360,000 at age 65. However, the first twin only saved $20,000, while the other twin saved a total of $76,000!

Three key components define the power of compounding:

- **Savings**: The more you save, the faster your wealth grows.
- **Time**: Early savings experience more rapid compounding than later contributions. Compounding's greatest impact occurs over longer periods (30 years or more).
- **Rate of Return**: A higher return accelerates your money's growth. At 2%, your wealth doubles every 35 years; at 4%, it doubles every 17 years; and at 8%, your wealth doubles every 9 years.

Returning to the UBC professor's scenario, opting for the daily $33,000 would give you approximately $1 million in a month. However, selecting the doubling route results in over $10 million on the last day alone, amassing over $21 million in total. This vividly demonstrates the astonishing power of compounding on an extreme scale.

Extra Credit:

Compounding also extends to life decisions. Some choices made today can either limit or open doors for future opportunities. For instance, a reckless decision like driving under the influence can lead to injuries, legal troubles, and challenges in securing future employment. Conversely, an extra course taken in university might lead to discovering new interests, meeting influential individuals, and unlocking unforeseen career pathways.

A famous example is Steve Jobs, who credited a calligraphy course during his university days for inspiring the diverse font options in Apple computers and his commitment to creating beautiful, not just practical computers.

Quotes to Ponder

"The time to save for the future is now. Thanks to compound interest, the earlier you start putting money away for the future, the more you will save." – Alexa Von Tobel, a 30-year-old author of Financially Forward

"People are reasonably good at estimating how things add up. But for compounding, which involves repeated multiplication, we fail to appreciate how quickly things grow." – Paul Romer, American economist

How to Use Debt

Once upon a time, there was a Donkey being driven along a road leading down the mountainside. Suddenly, it took it into its silly head to choose its own path. The Donkey could see its stall at the foot of the mountain, and to it, the quickest way down seemed to be over the edge of the nearest cliff. Just as it was about to leap over, its master caught it by the tail and tried to pull it back. But the stubborn Donkey would not yield and pulled with all its might.

"Very well," said its master, "go your way, you willful beast, and see where it leads you." With that, he let go, and the foolish Donkey tumbled head over heels down the mountainside and met its demise.

First things first: Debt is neither inherently good nor bad, but if used improperly, it can be disastrous.

In the fable above, the Donkey sought a shortcut, much like how some people use debt instead of patiently saving for their desired purchases.

Debt is essentially an obligation that Future You must fulfill. It represents someone, often a bank, giving you money now with the expectation that you will pay it back later. Not only must you repay the principal amount borrowed, but you'll also incur interest costs for the privilege of borrowing.

Over time, this interest can accumulate substantially, sometimes even doubling the original loan amount.

Here's some straightforward debt advice:

1. Begin by building up your chequing account to hold at least $1,000, and make sure it never dips below that threshold. If you don't have over $1,000 in your checking account, avoid obtaining a credit card or accumulating debt for any reason.
2. Once you have a steady financial base, consider getting a credit card, but only charge expenses you can already cover with your existing funds. Never carry a balance, and pay off the credit card in full every single month. I repeat: **NEVER carry a credit card balance**. Unfortunately, many people facing financial struggles have credit card debt they are struggling to repay.
3. Reserve debt for the purchase of investments. Never use debt to fund vacations, buy furniture, dine out, or for leisure activities.
4. Use debt judiciously when it can improve the future quality of your life, such as a mortgage for a house or an investment in a viable business opportunity.

Exercise caution with debt, as it can either significantly improve or severely hinder your financial wellbeing.

Quotes to Ponder

"Debt is like any other trap, easy enough to get into, but hard enough to get out of." – Henry Wheeler Shaw, writer and humorist

"Some debts are fun when you buy things, but not fun when you set about paying the debt back." – Ogden Nash, poet

"Debt can turn a free, happy person into a bitter human being." – Michael Mihalik, author

"Here is an equation worth remembering: Five dollars earned minus seven dollars spent equals an unhappy life." – Jon Morrison

Never Stop Learning

One day, a fox and a hedgehog were out for a walk. They engaged in a conversation about their respective strategies for avoiding capture by eagles.

The fox regaled the hedgehog with stories of how he had skillfully escaped from the clutches of eagles in various ways. He mentioned tactics like running into other animals' burrows, hiding in tall grass, or climbing trees and blending into the branches.

The hedgehog, on the other hand, had a different approach. He mentioned that he knew only one method, but it was a significant one. He would curl into a protective ball, relying on his prickly spines to deter any potential predators. Both animals debated the merits of their strategies, but neither could convincingly sway the other.

This fable is a favorite of mine because it underscores that there can be multiple solutions to a problem. While relying on one significant skill (akin to the hedgehog) can work, some aspects of life today are too complex. Things change rapidly, and there is always something new to discover. With some scientists predicting that today's young people might live to 120 years old in good health, the prospect of continued learning over the next 75 years is exciting to me.

Some individuals believe they'll be finished once they reach a specific financial milestone. In the 1980s, that benchmark was a million dollars, but today, it barely covers the cost of a home in many areas. So, is it $2 million? $3 million? The reality is, as you progress, new financial challenges will arise, whether it's saving up more money for new ventures or managing what you already have.

A more practical approach to finances is to accept that it's a lifelong journey. Currently, you're learning about saving, bank accounts, and spending. Next, you'll delve into topics like purchasing a car or a home, being a valuable employee, or negotiating a raise (when deserved, of course 😉). Later, you might explore buying a second home, starting a business, and managing employees. Eventually, you'll need to plan for retirement and consider how to pass on your wealth to loved ones or charitable causes.

This is not meant to overwhelm you. It's akin to the saying about how to eat an elephant—one bite at a time. The topic of money is enormous and you won't reach the end quickly as there will always be new challenges to tackle.

So, be patient, keep learning, and stay curious. Read, converse with people, listen to podcasts, and don't hesitate to seek advice. Speaking of which, let's explore the final essential chapter.

Quotes to Ponder

"There is only one way to eat an elephant: one bite at a time." – Desmond Tutu, famous African human rights activist

Please Ask for Advice

Once, there were two frogs who were close friends. One lived in a large, serene pond in the woods, where overhanging trees shielded it from disturbances. The other lived in a small, less desirable pool by a country road, where passing horses and wagons muddied the water and disrupted the tranquility.

One day, the frog from the larger pond invited the other to live with him, extolling the virtues of plenty of food, clean water, and undisturbed peace. However, the frog from the smaller pool declined the offer, content with its familiar surroundings. It preferred its own pond, despite the challenges.

The next time the frog from the larger pond came to visit, he couldn't find his friend. A bird living in a tree over the smaller pool delivered the unfortunate news.

"Too late," sang the bird. "Your friend is gone, run over by a wagon and taken away by a hawk."

"Alas!" lamented the frog from the larger pond. "If only he had heeded my advice, he might have been safe and happy now. But he insisted on his own way, and I have lost my friend."

The most successful people I've met have all sought help at some point. Whether it's from parents, relatives, teachers, mentors, or business associates, asking for help is not a sign of weakness. Instead, it's a demonstration of strength in recognizing that you don't know everything and are eager to learn.

Life is not about proving your intelligence; it's about becoming intelligent. Allow people into your life who want to help you, and you're more likely to achieve success. In the beginning, your parents might be your most valuable resource. If they haven't achieved financial success, consider reaching out to the parents of your friends. Invite them for coffee (your treat) and share your financial story to seek their advice.

Some areas where you might seek help include:

- Maximizing the use of chequing and savings accounts.
- Planning for taxes and handling unexpected financial challenges.
- Identifying optimal savings strategies as your income grows.
- Guidance on purchasing your first home, as they've already experienced it.
- Investment advice or recommendations on where to find financial guidance.

Remember, it's not a sign of weakness to seek advice. On the contrary, strength lies in having a supportive team around you who can help you make better decisions. Regardless of your intelligence, the collective wisdom of those around you can offer valuable insights and prevent you from repeating their past mistakes.

Quotes to Ponder

"Intelligent individuals learn from everything and every one; average people learn only from their experiences. The stupid already have all the answers." – Socrates, Greek philosopher

The Most Important Things to Remember

The hardest part of writing anything is deciding what's important and what's extra. What must be in the book and what can I leave out.

The topic of money has so many facets, that even for a professional like me, it can be overwhelming. So I wanted to end the book with the key things that I think are the most important.

First, you have some control over how things end up. You have the ability to make decisions that will improve or make things worse. You are not helpless. Your financial future isn't set in stone. You can make things better. It's about making progress...not about getting things perfect.

Second, there will be challenges. Managing finances is a lifelong process. There will be ups and downs. You will make mistakes but if you can minimize them, you will be OK. Everything is figureoutable.

Third, it takes work. I've never met a financially successful person who didn't put in time and effort. No one is an overnight success...you just don't see the hours, days, and years they've put into getting to where they are. Habits of hard work, resilience, diligence, and conscientiousness start now...you may not see the benefits of them in the short term, but when you look back, it will be obvious how you got to where you are.

Fourth, ask, ask, ask for help. No one is successful on their own. There are friends, mentors, advisors, books, podcasts, and articles from whom you can learn and improve. Financial success isn't about proving you are smart. It's about becoming smart.

I hope this book will help you to approach finances differently. Pay attention to your emotions. Make active choices about how you think. And never stop learning.

Edwin Palsma

Disclaimer

"This book is written by Edwin Palsma in his individual capacity and not as a registered representation of Raymond James Ltd. (RJL) or any of its affiliates. It expresses the opinions of the authors and not necessarily those of Raymond James Ltd. This book is provided as a general source of information and should not be considered personal investment advice or financial planning advice. It should not be construed as an offer or solicitation for the sale or purchase of any product and should not be considered tax advice. We are not tax advisors, and we recommend that clients seek independent advice from a professional advisor on tax-related matters. We recommend any individual seek independent advice from an investment advisor prior to making any investment decisions and from a professional accountant concerning tax-related matters. Statistics, factual data and other information are from sources RJL believes to be reliable, but their accuracy cannot be guaranteed. This book is furnished on the basis and understanding that Raymond James Ltd. or any of its affiliates are to be under no liability whatsoever in respect, therefore. This book may provide reference to third-party services. Raymond James Ltd. is not responsible for the availability of these external services, nor does Raymond James Ltd endorse, warrant, or guarantee the products, services or information described or offered. Commissions, trailing commissions, management fees and expenses all may be associated with mutual funds. Please read the prospectus before investing. Mutual funds are not guaranteed, their values change frequently, and past performance may not be repeated. Securities-related products and services are offered through Raymond James Ltd., Member - Canadian Investor Protection Fund. Insurance products and services products and services are offered through Raymond James Financial Planning Ltd., which is not a Member - Canadian Investor Protection Fund."